The Beauty of Holiness

By Linda Singletary

Dedication

For many years I heard Doris Pickering's name and knew she wrote materials for ladies' meetings, but it was not until 1993 that I actually met her. We found out that we had much in common and soon became good friends.

Doris served the Lord along with her husband, LeeRoy, for over 40 years. They served in the pastorate for 35 years and then in evangelism for 7 years. She wrote 32 books ladies ministry books, and started Christian Creation website to make her materials available to others. What a blessing she was to pastor's wives all across our country. I still hear her name mentioned in the churches where we visit.

When Doris found out I had written a few skits for ladies she encouraged me to put them together in a book, and she advertised them on her website. Later she encouraged me to do the same with my Bible studies.

In 1996, Doris asked me to speak at her ladies' retreat on the subject, "The Beauty of Holiness." It has taken me several years to put this study into book form but Doris is the inspiration behind this study.

The Lord took Doris home to heaven on February 20, 2006. I appreciate so much the encouragement she was to me over the years and I miss her very much.

Linda Singletary
2007

Psalm 96:9
"O worship the LORD in the beauty of holiness."

All scriptures in this book are taken from the King James Bible.

Other books by this author:

A Garden of Roses is Jesus

Being a Contented Christian

Being a Fruitful Christian

Being a Teachable Christian

How About Your Heart?

It's a Jungle Out There

Walk in the Spirit

Wanted! Godly Woman

Table of Contents

Lesson One

"O, To Be Beautiful"

"O, To Be Beautiful"

"...Rachel was beautiful and well favoured." Genesis 29:17

No doubt every woman has at some point in her life been dissatisfied with her looks and wished that she could be more beautiful. There is nothing wrong with being beautiful. Surveys have shown that there are advantages to being beautiful. The cute kid on the school playground usually gets selected before the ugly duckling. The pretty girl has no trouble getting volunteers to fix her flat tire. The handsome guy often gets preferences in the job market. While these things may not be fair, they are a fact of life.

In the book of Genesis, Rachel won the heart of Jacob because she was beautiful. From the first time Jacob laid eyes on Rachel, before he even knew her, he loved her and was willing to work seven years to make her his wife. We know the story of how her father, Laban, deceived Jacob and gave him her sister, Leah, who evidently was not very beautiful. In Genesis 29:17 Leah is referred to as being "tender eyed." Because of Jacob's love for Rachel, he agreed to work another seven years to make her his wife. This love, which began because of her beauty, lasted a lifetime, for until Rachel's death she was Jacob's favorite wife and her two sons, Joseph and Benjamin, were his favorite children.

Just as there is nothing wrong with being beautiful, neither is there anything wrong with trying to look our best. As Christians, we are representatives of the Lord and it is important that we make a good showing for Him. Being homely does not make a person more spiritual, and being unkept is a very poor testimony that can even turn others away.

A married woman should also try to look her best for her husband. After years of marriage it is easy to become lax in the matter of our appearance around our husbands. Women dress up to go to work where they are around other men, but at home they often look very slouchy. When you go out with your husband, don't let him ever be ashamed of the way you look. Make him proud to introduce you as his wife. Proverbs 12:4 warns "...she that maketh ashamed is as rottenness in his bones.

Mirror, Mirror on the Wall; Who is the Fairest of Them All?

The problem is that some women become obsessed with their looks. Insecurities within themselves may cause them to become over-concerned with their looks. They may believe that if they are beautiful on the outside no one will notice what's on the inside. Women often use some very drastic means trying to improve their looks.

Plastic surgery is no longer reserved for correcting serious imperfections but has become an everyday practice for vain people who are never satisfied with their looks. Some women seem to be addicted to plastic surgery and have it done on a regular basis. Sometimes they end up looking worse than they did before they started. Botox treatments and skin peels are also becoming more popular every day.

Being the most beautiful woman in the room or winning a beauty contest does not make one a better person. Those women who are obsessed with outward beauty might benefit from spending a little less time on the face and a little more time on the heart. Proverbs 31:30 tells us, "Favor is deceitful, and beauty is vain: but the woman that **feareth the LORD**, she shall be praised."

Any Old Barn Can Use a Little Paint Now and Then!

Though this virtuous woman in Proverbs 31 feared the Lord, she also seemed to be concerned about her appearance for we read in verse 22, "She maketh herself coverings of tapestry, her clothing is silk and purple." While she was making herself warm clothing to prepare for the winter, she certainly did use the most beautiful fabrics to do so. What we wear is very important to our appearance. Clothes should be clean and neatly pressed, but they need not be expensive to look nice. We once did a fashion show at our ladies' retreat and all of the clothes were purchased at thrift stores or yard sales. The models spent under $10 for their complete outfits, including shoes, and it would surprise you at how lovely each one looked.

Wearing clothes that properly fit your body and your personality can be a big boost to making you look good. Just because something is "the rage of the age" does not mean that it will add to your beauty, and you can waste a lot of money buying fads that will be out of style next season. Stick with a style that fits you well and add small accessories to keep it up to date. How often have you seen someone at the mall, dressed in the latest fashion, but looking ridiculous because the outfit just did not fit?

We read in I Timothy 2:9-10, "In like manner also, that women adorn themselves in **modest** apparel, with shamefacedness and sobriety; not with broided hair, or gold, or pearls, or costly array; but (which becometh women professing godliness) with good works." According to Webster's dictionary the word modest includes several things-- moderate, decent, unpretentious.

To be moderate means not going to extremes. Decent means to be adequately clothed so that there is no need for shame. Unpretentious suggests not being too showy. I don't believe these verses are saying that it is wrong to braid your hair or to wear jewelry and expensive clothing, but rather that the emphasis should be on something far more important—a right spirit before God. I Peter 3:3-4 says much the same thing, "Whose adorning let it not be that outward adorning of plaiting the hair, and of wearing of gold, or of putting on of apparel; but let it be the hidden man of the heart, in that which is not corruptible, even the ornament of a meek and quiet spirit, which is in the sight of God of great price."

You're Not Getting Older, You're Getting Better!

Beauty is often equated with youth and women spend vast amounts of money on all kinds of **miracle** creams and lotions, hoping that they can remove a few wrinkles or at least prevent some from appearing. Wouldn't it be great if these were really the miracles they are advertised to be? It would also have been wonderful if Ponce de Leon could have discovered that "fountain of youth" he was searching for many years ago there in Florida. Sinful habits such as smoking, drinking and using drugs can cause premature aging and destroy a woman's good looks. Wrong attitudes such as being bitter and unforgiving can also cause one to age.

Since I am now an older lady I like these old sayings, "you're not getting older, you're getting better," and "you're like a good wine, you've improved with age." I've seen women that have improved with age and are prettier than they were in their youth because they have learned how to take care of themselves by wearing the right clothes, finding a flattering hairstyle and properly using makeup. Many older women are still very beautiful because they have developed an inner beauty and they just seem to glow. Proverbs 16:31 says, "The hoary (white or gray) head is a crown of glory, if it be found in the way of righteousness." Proverbs 20:29 says, "The glory of young men is their strength: and the **beauty** of old men is the gray head." I'm sure the same thing could be said for women as for men.

The Battle of the Bulge!

Weight is another thing we think of in connection with beauty. Most people think a woman must be thin to be beautiful, but some woman, especially young women, go to extremes with thinness. Bulimia and anorexia are two dangerous eating disorders that we hear a lot about today.

These can occur when people become over concerned with thinness. Of course, we know that being greatly overweight can also affect our health. Once again, moderation seems to be the solution to both of these problems. Proverbs 23:1-2 warns, "When thou sittest to eat with a ruler, consider diligently what is before thee: and put a knife to thy throat, if thou be a man **given to appetite**." To eat the right food in moderation on a daily basis is much wiser than overindulging one day and dieting the next. Yoyo dieting does not produce lasting results. You must change your eating habits to maintain weight loss. Take care of your body; it belongs to the Lord. I Corinthians 3:16-17, "Know ye not that **ye are the temple of God**, and that the Spirit of God dwelleth in you? If any man defile the temple of God, him shall God destroy." any people die each year as a result from both overeating and from starvation.

How Does God View Beauty?

Another saying we often hear is "beauty is in the eye of the beholder." This is very true for what one person sees as beautiful may differ from what someone else thinks is beautiful. On a trip to Thailand my husband and I visited the Karen Longneck tribe where the women wear metal rings around their necks because this is considered beautiful by their tribe. The first rings are put on when the girls are very young and as they grow older more rings are added. The rings cannot be removed and, in Thailand where it is very hot, these women often develop a serious rash. The rings appear to stretch the neck, but actually they push down on the ribs causing the women to be susceptible to respiratory diseases. This practice may be considered strange and destructive to us, but it is beautiful to the Karen Longneck tribe.

The Lord loves beautiful things. Didn't He create a beautiful world for us to live in? I am amazed as I travel around our great country at all the beauty I see. There are such contrasts of landscapes and yet each one has its own beauty.

God instructed the Israelites to make beautiful things for both the tabernacle in the wilderness and for the temple in Jerusalem. The Israelites were given detailed instructions as to what kind of materials to use. They were to use the best and nothing was left to chance. Ezra 7:27, "Blessed be the LORD God of our fathers, which hath put such a thing as this in the king's heart, to **beautify** the house of the LORD which is in Jerusalem:" Jerusalem, the city of our great God, is spoken of in Lamentations 2:15 as "The perfection of **beauty**, the joy of the whole earth."

Man's views and God's view on beauty may not always be in agreement, but we know that God's view is the only one that really matters. Isaiah 53:2, in speaking of the coming Saviour said, "...he hath no form nor comeliness; and when we shall see him, there is no **beauty** that we should desire him." Christ may not be beautiful to the world but He is beautiful to God and He should be beautiful to us.

As we grow in the Lord we should be able to say as David did in Psalm 27:4, "One thing have I desired of the LORD, that will I seek after; that I may dwell in the house of the LORD all the days of my life, to **behold the beauty of the LORD**, and to inquire in his temple." To behold the beauty of the Lord was evidently very important to David for this verse says it was the one thing that he desired. David sought this beauty of the Lord by dwelling in the house of the Lord. Does this not indicate that being faithful to God's house should be very important to us?

The big question then is "how does God see me?" Am I beautiful to Him?

Questions

1. To make our husband ashamed is as what? Prov.12:4
   _____

2. Where in the Bible do we read about the virtuous woman? _____

3. List three things that are included in the word modest.
   _____

4. I Peter 3:4 instructs us to adorn ourselves with a "_____and
   _____ spirit.

5. What does the word "hoary" found in Prov.16:31 mean? _____

6. Prov. 23:1-2 says that if you have are given to overeating you should do what?
   _____

7. According to Isa. 53:2, was Christ considered beautiful by the world?
   _____

8. David said in Ps. 27:4 that the thing he desired was to "..dwell in the house of
   the Lord" and to "behold the _____."

Lesson Two

"Beautiful for Thee, Lord"

"Beautiful for Thee, Lord"

"And let the beauty of the LORD our God be upon us:" Psalm 90:17

We are often under the impression that if things look good on the outside that is all that matters, but that is definitely not true. Christ admonished the Pharisees in Matthew 23:25-26, "Woe unto you, scribes and Pharisees, hypocrites! for ye make clean the outside of the cup and of the platter, but within they are full of extortion and excess. Thou blind Pharisee, **cleanse first that which is within** the cup and platter, that the outside of them may be clean also."

So many women are going through life, perfectly groomed and outwardly appearing to have everything under control, when in reality on the inside they are like a volcano waiting to erupt. We might be able to fool those around us but the Lord knows what is going on inside of us.

You Can't Fix the Engine by Polishing the Hood!

What is most important to you, being beautiful in the eyes of man or being beautiful in the eyes of God? How can we be beautiful in the eyes of God? The best advice for that is "Don't spend so much time caring for the outside that you neglect the inside." I Samuel 16:7 says, "...for the LORD seeth not as man seeth; for man looketh on the **outward appearance**, but the LORD looketh on the **heart**."

The book of Proverbs offers a few suggestions as to how we might improve our outward as well as our inward beauty. Proverbs 15:13 says, "A **merry heart** maketh a **cheerful countenance**." A merry heart is good for our health as well as our countenance. Proverbs 17:22, "A **merry heart** doeth good like a medicine: but a broken spirit drieth the bones." Proverbs 12:25, "Heaviness in the heart of man maketh it stoop: but a good word maketh it glad."

A broken spirit and a heavy heart lead to depression, and depression is often reflected in our countenance and can be hazardous to our health. Praise is the best antidote available for depression. When you are depressed try reading the book of Psalms, which is full of verses on praise. Psalm 69:30, "I will **praise** the name of God with a song, and will magnify him with thanksgiving."

Praise is not dependent upon the circumstances that surround us. To praise the Lord in spite of how we might feel is like priming a pump with a little water to produce more water. As we begin to praise the Lord, He will produce praise in our heart. Psalm 4: 7, "Thou hast put **gladness in my heart**, more than in the time that their corn and their wine increased." Praise can also produce peace and peace in the heart puts a smile on the face. Psalm 4:8, "I will both lay me down in **peace**, and sleep: for thou, Lord, only makest me dwell in safety." Follow this advice and help reduce those lines caused by worry!

Collagen Injections or Lips Dedicated to God?

Big, full lips are "in" these days. Some woman are getting Collagen injections to produce this look, but God's Word offers some alternatives for developing beautiful lips. Psalm 45:1-2 tells us that when our mouth is dedicated to the Lord, our tongue will become "the pen of a ready writer" because "**grace** is poured into thy **lips**." With grace in our lips we will be able to speak as Christ did in Luke 4:22. "And all bare him witness, and wondered at the **gracious words** which proceeded out of his mouth."

Proverbs 20:15 speaks of how the Lord values lips that speak knowledge, "There is gold, and a multitude of rubies: but the **lips of knowledge are a precious jewel**." Proverbs 22:17-18, "Bow down thine ear, and hear the words of the wise, and apply thine heart unto my knowledge. For it is a **pleasant thing** if thou keep them within thee; they shall withal be **fitted in thy lips**." We must first have these wise words implanted in our heart if they are to be fitted in our lips. The Word of God is where we find these wise words. David prayed in Psalm 51:15, "O Lord, open thou my **lips**; and my mouth shall shew forth thy **praise**."

Proverbs 5 warns us of the deception of the strange or wicked woman and says in verses 3-4, "For the **lips** of a **strange woman** drop as an honeycomb, and her mouth is smoother than oil: but her end is bitter as wormwood, sharp as a twoedged sword." Proverbs 2:16-18 tells us that she "**flattereth with her words**" but to follow her leads down a deadly path.

O, Those Beautiful Eyes, Those Great Big, Beautiful Eyes!
When I met my husband, many, long years ago, one of the first things that I noticed was his long, thick eyelashes. I was so happy that, out of our three children, it was our daughter that inherited them. While I still think his eyelashes are beautiful, my husband often complains about what a pain they are. I guess we're never satisfied.

Eyes reveal so much about a person. You can often detect that a person is not feeling well by looking at his eyes. Messages are conveyed with the eyes--a raised eyebrow, a wink, a squint--can each send a message. We flirt and we tease with our eyes. Much evil can be taken in through our eyes. What do your eyes read or what do you watch on TV? Proverbs 6:25 gives a warning to men about a woman's eyes, "Lust not after her beauty in thine heart; neither let her take thee with her **eyelids**."

Eyes can be used for many good things. David said in Psalm 25:15, "**Mine eyes are ever toward the Lord**" and in Psalm 121:1-2 we read, "I will lift up mine **eyes** unto the hills, from whence cometh my help. My help cometh from the LORD, which made heaven and earth." If you want to have beautiful eyes keep them focused on the Lord!

Pretty Feet!

It was August when I went to the hospital to deliver my second child and I had been wearing sandals all summer. I remember being embarrassed about my dry, cracked heels. I wish I would have known about the foot care product, Pretty Feet, which might have made them look better. In Isaiah 52: 7, the Lord tells us a how to make our feet beautiful to Him. "How **beautiful** upon the mountains are the **feet** of him that bringeth good tidings, that publisheth **peace**; that bringeth good tidings of good, that publisheth **salvation**..."

This must be a very important verse because it is repeated in Romans 10:15, "How **beautiful** are the **feet** of them that preach the **gospel of peace**, and bring glad tidings of good things!" Women often paint their toenails, wear pretty shoes and sometimes even add rings and bracelets to make their feet look beautiful, but the best beauty application for our feet is to go to others and tell them the good news of salvation which will assure them of eternal peace. Ephesians 6:15, "And your **feet** shod with the preparation of the **gospel of peace**."

The opposite side of this coin is found in Proverbs 6:12-14, "A naughty person, a wicked man, **walketh with a froward mouth**. He winketh with his eyes, he **speaketh with his feet**, he teacheth with his fingers; frowardness is in his heart, he deviseth mischief continually; he soweth discord." A gospel chorus we sometimes sing says, "Your walk talks more than your talk talks." In other words—actions speak louder than words.

Cauliflower Ears!

A cauliflower ear is an ear deformed from injury or excessive growth. No one wants cauliflower ears. When my second son was born he was a very big baby and as a result of his position in the womb, his ear was completely folded over. There just was not enough room in there for him. I was quite disturbed and wished that he could have been a girl thinking that his ear could at least be covered with hair. I supposed he would have to have surgery to repair this deformity, but how thankful I was that in a few days the ear started to unfold and was soon back to normal.

One of the Old Testament rituals was that of putting blood on an object that was to be consecrated to the Lord. In Levitcus 8 we read about Moses taking the blood of a ram and putting it on the tip of Aaron's right ear. Though we no longer observe this practice today, we do need to consecrate our ears to the Lord. We need to be careful about the things we listen to and we need to always listen to the Lord.

Jeremiah 9:20 speaks to the women at the temple gate saying, "Yet **hear** the word of the LORD, O ye women, and let your **ear** receive the word of his mouth, and **teach** your daughters wailing, and every one her neighbour lamentation." As women we are often tempted to listen to gossip and then sometimes tempted to repeat what we have heard. This can get us into trouble, but when we listen to God we can confidently repeat what He tells us, and we should especially repeat those things to our daughters and our neighbors.

Psalm 78:1 says, "**Give ear**, O my people, to my law; **incline your ears** to the words of my mouth." Proverbs 15:31 says, "The **ear that heareth** the reproof of life abideth among the wise." Don't be like "the deaf adder that stoppeth her ear" which is mentioned in Psalm 58:4. "Oh, be careful little ears what you hear!

Lovely Hands!

The Bible does not mention beautiful hands, but it does speak of clean hands as being pleasing to the Lord. Psalm 18:20, "...according to the **cleanness of my hands** hath he recompensed me." Psalm 24:3-4, "Who shall ascend into the hill of the LORD? or who shall stand in his holy place? He that hath **clean hands**, and a pure heart."

Another use of our hands that would be pleasing to the Lord is that of folding or lifting our hands in prayer. I Timothy 2:8, "I will therefore that men pray everywhere, lifting up **holy hands**." Clean and holy hands belong to those who have a clean heart because their sins have been confessed and forgiven. If our prayers are to be heard our hands and heart must be clean. Psalm 66:18, "If I **regard iniquity** in my heart, **the Lord will not hear me**:"

To clap our hands is a sign of approval and joy. Psalm 47:1 says, "O clap your **hands**, all ye people; shout unto God with the voice of triumph."

Of course, many good works are accomplished with the hands. The hands of the virtuous woman in Proverbs 31 must have been beautiful hands in God's sight, for her hands are praised several times in that chapter. Verse 13 says she "…**worketh willingly with her hands**." Verse 16 tells us, "…with the fruit of her **hands** she planteth a vineyard."

In verses 19-20 we read, "She layeth her **hands** to the spindle, and her **hands** hold the distaff. She stretcheth out her **hand** to the poor; yea, she reacheth forth her **hands** to the needy." This lady had very industrious hands that she wisely used to serve the Lord. The chapter closes in verse 31 by saying, "Give her of the fruit of **her hands**; and let her own works praise her in the gates."

Our key verse for this lesson, Psalm 90:17, says, "And let the **beauty of the LORD our God be upon us.**" This verse goes on to say "and establish thou the work of our **hands** upon us; yea, the work of our **hands** establish thou it." I believe this is speaking of the anointing of the Holy Spirit. If my work for the Lord is to endure I must have the anointing of the Holy Spirit upon my life.

Our prayer should be, "Lord, make me beautiful for Thee."

Questions

1. I Sam. 16:7 tells us that man looks on the _____ but the Lord looks _____.

2. If we dedicate our mouth to the Lord what will He pour into our lips? _____ Ps. 45:2

3. Prov. 2:16 mentions the "strange woman" who does what with her words? _____

4. According to Rom. 10:15 what makes your feet beautiful? _____ _____

5. In order to stand in God's holy place, we are told in Ps. 24:3-4 that we need _____ and a _____.

6. What were some of the things that the virtuous women of Proverbs 31 used her hands for? (vs. 13) _____ (vs.16) _____ (vs.19) _____ (vs. 20) _____

7. What does Prov. 15:31 call the person who hears the reproof of life?_____

8. In Prov. 31:31, the virtuous woman's good works were called "the fruit of her_____."

Lesson Three

"The Value of Holiness"

"The Value of Holiness"

"...be in behaviour as becometh holiness," Titus 2:3

These above words, "be in behaviour as becometh **holiness**" were written to the aged women, but they certainly should be a goal for all Christian women. At times this might seem like an unattainable goal, but nonetheless it should be a goal that we strive to reach.

I Peter 1:15-16 instructs us, "But as he which hath called you is **holy**, so be ye **holy** in all manner of conversation; because it is written, **Be ye holy; for I am holy**." Peter is quoting from the book of Leviticus where God is instructing Moses and the Israelites on what they were and were not to do, and says in Leviticus 11:44, ...**ye shall be holy; for I am holy**." Of course, we know that only God is absolutely holy, but our desire should be to be like Him.

David said in Psalm 17:15, "I shall be satisfied, when I awake, with thy likeness." In Hannah's prayer of rejoicing in I Samuel 2:2 after God had given her a baby son, Samuel, she sang, "**There is none holy as the LORD**." While we will never in this life be able to be as holy as God, we should still continue to work on being holy.

The verse I have chosen as my verse for this year, 2007, is II Corinthians 7:1, "Having therefore these promises, dearly beloved, let us cleanse ourselves from all filthiness of the flesh and spirit, **perfecting holiness**, in the fear of God." It takes a lot of practice to perfect something, so while I do not expect to become perfect, I do want to work on it or practice being holy. The key to doing this is found in the last phrase of this verse, "in the fear of God." To fear God is to believe and obey God. When I really believe God I will want to obey Him, and when I obey Him I will be practicing holiness.

The word holy means whole, entire, complete, sound, unimpaired, perfect. In the Old Testament, things or places that were referred to as holy were those that were sanctified or set apart for a sacred purpose. The opposite of the word holy would be common, unclean or profane. Leviticus 21:6, "They shall be **holy** unto their God, and not **profane** the name of their God." God set apart the Israelites, His chosen people, to be a holy people. They had a special relationship to God Jehovah and because He was holy in character they were to be holy in character. If we are saved we, too, have a special relationship with God. I Thessalonians 4:7, "For God hath not called us unto uncleaness, but unto **holiness**."

The Holy Place

In the book of Exodus, God told Moses to build the tabernacle--the holy place where God would dwell. Exodus 25:8, "And let them make me a sanctuary; that I may dwell among them." God gave Moses explicit instructions for building this tabernacle and for all of the furnishings that would go into the tabernacle. Inside the tabernacle there were to be two holy rooms. Exodus 26:33, "...and the vail shall divide unto you between the **holy place** and the **most holy**."

The Holy Garments

Before the building actually began, God chose Aaron to become the high priest and Aaron's sons to be the priests who would minister in the tabernacle. God told Moses in Exodus 28:2-3, "And thou shalt make **holy garments** for Aaron thy brother for glory and for **beauty**. And thou shalt speak unto all that are wise hearted, whom I have filled with the spirit of wisdom, that they may make Aaron's garments to **consecrate** him, that he may minister unto me in the priest's office."

The Israelites, under the direction of the priests, were to carry out many laws and rituals of holiness. To perform these rituals the priests were to wear the holy garments, but before they put on those garments they were to cleanse themselves. Exodus 30:19-20, "For Aaron and his sons shall **wash** their hands and their feet thereat: when they go into the tabernacle of the congregation, they shall wash with water, that they die not; or when they come near to the altar to minister, to burn offering made by fire unto the LORD."

The Holy Ointment

When the tabernacle was completed God told Moses in Exodus 30:25-30, "And thou shalt make it an oil of **holy ointment**, and ointment compound after the art of the apothecary: it shall be an **holy anointing oil**. And thou shalt anoint the tabernacle of the congregation therewith, and the ark of the testimony, and the table and all his vessels, and the candlestick and his vessels, and the altar of incense, and the altar of burnt offering with all his vessels, and the laver and his foot. And thou shalt sanctify them, that they may be **most holy**: whatsoever toucheth them shall be **holy**. And thou shalt anoint Aaron and his sons, and consecrate them, that they may minister unto me in the priest's office." This holy anointing oil was to be used for no other purpose and not to be poured upon any other person and it was not to be reproduced. (Exodus 30:31-33)

The Holy Day

God had also set apart the seventh day of the week as a sabbath or holy day when the people were to rest and do no work. Exodus 31:14, "Ye shall keep the sabbath therefore; for it is **holy** unto you; every one that defileth it shall surely be put to death: for whosoever doeth any work therein, that soul shall be cut off from among his people."

The Holy Lamb

It would have been wonderful if the Israelites would have lived up to the holiness God had outlined for them, but He knew that they would not. God made provision for their failures by allowing them to offer blood sacrifices when they had sinned. The external holiness required by the ceremonial laws represented the spiritual holiness required by God. Because God is truly holy, He cannot tolerate sin. When the Israelites sinned, and then offered a sacrifice, they were acknowledging their dependence upon God. Just as the Israelites could not go without sinning, neither can we go without sinning today.

However, it is so much easier for us to confess our sins than it was for the Israelites. We do not have to offer a blood sacrifice each time we sin as the Israelites did. Christ, the perfect Lamb of God, became our once for all sacrifice when He willingly gave His life on Calvary's cross.

In Hebrews 9, we read about the tabernacle and the first covenant and how Christ was the fulfillment of that covenant. Hebrews 9:24-26, "For Christ is not entered into the holy places made with hands, which are the figures of the true; but into heaven itself, now to appear in the presence of God for us: nor yet that he should **offer himself often**, as the high priest entereth into the holy place every year with blood of others; for then must he often have suffered since the foundation of the world: but now **once** in the end of the world hath he appeared to put away sin by the **sacrifice of himself**."

When Christ came in the flesh to this earth He lived an absolute holy life and this distinguished Him from all mere human beings. When we receive Christ as our Saviour, we are accepting Him as our Perfect Sacrifice. Through Jesus Christ we have immediate access to the Mercy Seat, and by merely confessing our sins to God we can have complete forgiveness. I John 1:9, "If we confess our sins, he is faithful and just to **forgive** us our sins, and to **cleanse** us from all unrighteousness." This seems like such a simple task and yet we often fail to take advantage of God's forgiveness and continue to live sinful and unholy lives.

The Holy Life

Separation from the World

It appears that most Christians today believe that holiness is not important and they have no desire to live a holy life. They feel that all that matters is that they are saved and have a ticket to heaven. They look like the world in the way they dress, talk like the world, go to the same places the world goes and do the same things the world does. They sometimes think they can win the world by living like the world.

This idea is contrary to what God's Word has to say. God told the Israelites in Leviticus 20:26, "And ye shall be **holy** unto me: for I the LORD am **holy**, and have severed you from other people, that ye should be mine." Paul told the church at Corinth in II Corinthians 6:17, "Wherefore come out from among them, and be ye separate, saith the Lord, and touch not the unclean thing; and I will receive you." Hebrews 12:14 says, "Follow peace with all men, and **holiness**, without which no man shall see the Lord."

Those around us should be able to see a difference in our lives and by that know that we belong to God. Paul, in writing to the Thessalonians, said in I Thessalonians 2:10, "Ye are witnesses, and God also, how **holily** and justly and unblameably we behaved ourselves among you that believe."

Separation Unto God

While holiness does include separating from sin and worldly practices, doing that alone does not make one holy. In some Muslim countries the women never go out in public without completely covering their bodies including their faces, but are they holy? No, they are not. They do this to appease a false god.

Living in a monastery, cut off from the rest of the world, does not make one holy. Neither does living by a set of rules and regulations--a bunch of do's and don'ts— automatically make one holy. To remove all the sinful things from our life and not to replace them with God and His Word will leave you a void and empty Christian. Holiness begins in the heart as we separate ourselves unto God.

Paul said in Romans 1:1 that he was called to be an apostle and "**separated unto the gospel of God.**" The Lord told the church in Antioch in Acts 13:2, "**Separate me** Barnabas and Saul **for the work whereunto I have called them.**" This was a formal separation where the church put their stamp of approval on these men and their ministries. This is what churches do today when they ordain a man to the ministry.

As Christian women we do not need a special calling or a setting apart by our church in order to separate ourselves unto God. You can do this by keeping your sins confessed, avoiding the paths of sin, placing yourself under God's control and dedicating yourself to Him on a daily basis.

In Romans 6:19-22 we read, "...even so now **yield** your members servants to righteousness unto **holiness.** For when ye were the servants of sin, ye were free from righteousness. What fruit had ye then in those things whereof ye are now ashamed? for the end of those things is death. But now being made free from sin, and become servants to God, ye have your fruit unto **holiness**, and the end everlasting life."

Getting to know God
If you have a desire to separate yourself unto the Lord then you must spend time with the Lord. The more time you spend with the Lord the better you will get to know Him, and the more like Him you will become--the more holy you will become. One of my favorite verses is Philippians 3:10 and it gives us three steps to knowing the Lord. **"That I may know him, and..."**

"the power of his resurrection"
If it were not for the resurrection, Christ's death on the cross would have been to no avail. By His resurrection He became victorious over death and provided a way of salvation for us. When we receive Him as our Saviour we are experiencing "the power of His resurrection" but this is just the beginning to knowing the Lord. We must spend lots of time with the Lord to get to know the Lord.

When I married my husband on August 19, 1960, I thought I knew him, but now after more than forty-six years, I am still discovering things about him. For years I made soft cookies the way my kids liked them. One day after they had all left home, I over-baked a batch of cookies. They were so hard that I almost threw them away. When my husband tasted one he remarked that these were the best cookies I had ever made. It took me over twenty years to find out how my husband liked his cookies, but we have had hard cookies ever since.

Through the years I have learned many things about my husband and gotten to know him so much better than I did when I married him. Although I loved my husband very much when I married him, I can truly say that I love him more today than I did then. We have gone through both good and bad times, and both have been used to strengthen our love for each other. The same can be said for my relationship with the Lord. Salvation was just the beginning of that relationship.

"the fellowship of his sufferings"

Christ so willingly suffered on the cross to provide salvation for us and I believe that the sufferings we go through in this life teach us to appreciate His suffering for us. Suffering comes in different ways to different people but all of us will experience some suffering in this life. If we accept the suffering that comes our way as being God's will, then through the suffering, we can be strengthened and grow in the Lord. We can use our trials as a time of fellowshipping with the Lord or we can grumble, complain and become a bitter and miserable person.

I Peter 1:7, "That the **trial of your faith**, being much more precious than of gold that perisheth, though it be tried with fire, might be found unto praise and honour and glory at the appearing of Jesus Christ." As the fire purifies the silver and gold and makes it beautiful and valuable, so do the fiery trials we go through purify us and make us beautiful and valuable to the Lord. I Peter 4:13, "But rejoice, inasmuch as ye are **partakers of Christ's sufferings**, that, when his glory shall be revealed, ye may be glad also with exceeding joy."

I have had very little suffering in my lifetime but what I have had has brought me closer to the Lord and helped me to know Him in a better way. In 1967, my husband had pancreatic cancer and was given little hope of survival. While he was in the hospital I, too, was in the hospital giving birth to a baby girl. This was a difficult time both physically and financially, for we had very poor insurance and very little money to pay the bills. We learned to "lean upon the Lord" and He miraculously brought us through. Not only did He pay the bills in a very short time, He also gave healing to my husband. As I look back on those days I certainly would not want to go through them again, but I thank the Lord that I learned to love both my husband and the Lord more as a result of that suffering.

"being made conformable unto his death"

As we get to know the Lord better, first by salvation and second by suffering, we are being made conformable to His death. When we really get to know the Lord we will become more like Him and less like the world. We read in Romans 12:2, "And be not conformed to this world: but be ye transformed by the renewing of your mind, that ye may prove what is that good, and acceptable, and perfect will of God."

When we become so like Him, His will, no matter what it might be, will become our will. Before His death Jesus prayed in the garden of Gethsemane, "O my Father, if it be possible, let this cup pass from me: nevertheless not as I will, but as thou wilt." (Matthew 26:39) As we become conformed unto his death we, too, will be able to pray this prayer--not my will but thy will!

Though, in this life we will never reach perfection and never be as holy as God, we can live a holy life by dedicating ourselves completely to the Lord. This dedication is not a onetime act but something that we do each day. Romans 12:1, "I beseech you therefore, brethren, by the mercies of God, that ye present your bodies a living sacrifice, **holy**, acceptable unto God, which is your reasonable service."

Questions:

1. What did David say in Ps. 17:15 would cause him to be satisfied?
   _____

2. According to II Cor. 7:1, how can we perfect holiness in our life?
   _____

3. Who is the once for all sacrifice spoken of in Heb. 9:24-26?
   _____

4. What are the two types of separation mentioned in this lesson?
   Separation from the _____
   Separation unto _____

5. What are the three steps to knowing the Lord found in Phil. 3:10?
   (1)_____
   (2)_____
   (3) _____

6. What did Jesus pray in Matt. 26:39? _____

7. How does Rom. 12:1 tell us to present ourselves to God?
   _____

Lesson Four

"Come and Worship"

"Come and Worship"

"O come, let us worship and bow down: let us kneel before the LORD our maker."
Psalm 95:6

<u>Webster's 1828 Dictionary of the English Language</u> defines worship as "the act of paying divine honors to the Supreme Being; or the reverence and homage paid to him in religious exercise, consisting in adoration, confession, prayer, thanksgiving and the like." This old dictionary gives a biblical definition of worship, but we know that worship can be directed at many different gods, people or objects.

Only God Jehovah, however, is truly worthy of worship. Revelation 4:11, "**Thou art worthy, O Lord**, to receive glory and honour and power: for thou hast created all things, and for thy pleasure they are and were created." We were created for the purpose of worshipping and glorifying God and yet, how often do we really worship Him?

My good friend, Carolyn Pace, has along with her husband, Tom, been a missionary in Peru for over forty years. Several years ago Carolyn gave an excellent definition of the word worship. She said that **worship is giving God our undivided attention.** So often we go through the motions of worship but we are not worshipping because our thoughts are racing in many other directions. We may think that following certain rituals or orders of ceremony is worship, but that in itself is not worship. True worship must come from the heart.

Examples of Worship

The Old Testament gives us many examples of worship--some good and some bad. The first thing that Noah did when he got off of the ark was to build an altar and worship God with a burnt offering. (Genesis 8:20) Abraham obeyed God and took his son, Isaac to the mountains of Moriah to make a sacrifice of worship. He was willing to offer Isaac as a burnt offering, but believed that God would "**provide himself a lamb,**" and God did. When Abraham's servant, Eliezer, went in search of a wife for Isaac, Genesis 24:26 tells us that when he found Rebekah, "the man bowed down his head and **worshipped** the LORD."

The Israelites worshipped when God sent Moses and Aaron to deliver them from Egyptian bondage. They worshipped when the death angel smote the Egyptians and "passed over the houses of the children of Israel." (Exodus 12:27) It was not long, however, before they forgot God's blessings and deliverance and worshipped a molten calf. In Exodus 32:8 we read, "They have turned aside quickly out of the way which I commanded them: they have made them a molten calf, and have **worshipped** it, and have sacrificed thereunto, and said, These be thy gods, O Israel, which have brought thee up out of the land of Egypt."

As the Israelites journeyed through the heathen lands God told them in Exodus 34:13-14, "But ye shall destroy their altars, break their images, and cut down their groves: for thou shalt **worship no other god**: for the LORD, whose name is Jealous, is a jealous God." Just as God was not willing to share the Israelites' worship with that of strange gods, He does not want to share our worship of other things today.

Neither does God want us to worship the things that He has created. Deuteronomy 4:19, "And lest thou lift up thine eyes unto heaven, and when thou seest the sun, and the moon, and the stars, even all the host of heaven, shouldest be driven to **worship** them, and serve them..." We hear about many "new age" nature worshippers today. Romans 1:25 warns about this, "Who changed the truth of God into a lie, and **worshipped** and served the creature more than the Creator, who is blessed for ever."

David was a man of worship and he worshipped at what might be considered some strange times. After the death of his baby son, II Samuel 12:20 tells us, "Then David arose from the earth, and washed, and anointed himself, and changed his apparel, and came into the house of the LORD, and **worshipped**." This type of worship reveals his fear of the Lord and his acceptance of God's will. In II Samuel 15 when his son, Absalom, conspired against him, David worshipped.

Solomon, the wisest man who ever lived, in spite of God's warnings in I Kings 9, forsook the true God to worship the false gods of his many heathen wives. Many of Israel's kings did the same thing and brought God's judgment upon the nation. We are often quick to criticize them for their sin of worshipping idols, yet many times we are guilty of much the same sin when we allow things to become more important than God in our lives.

Elements of Worship

Sacrifice
Burnt offerings or sacrifices were an important element in Old Testament

worship. The Israelites offered blood sacrifices when they had sinned. They also offered other sacrifices such as thanksgiving and peace offerings. Since Christ became our once for all sacrifice we are no longer required to make burnt sacrifices. Hebrews 10:14, "For by **one offering** he hath perfected for ever them that are sanctified."

The Bible does mention other types of sacrifice that we can use to worship God today. Hebrews 13:15 says, "By him therefore let us offer the **sacrifice of praise** to God continually, that is, the **fruit of our lips** giving thanks to his name." In Philippians 4:18 Paul commends the church at Philippi for giving to him and his missionary ministry and calls their gifts "an odour of a sweet smell, a **sacrifice acceptable, well pleasing to God**."

The Philippians were not a wealthy people but they sacrificed to give to Paul so that he could take the gospel to those who had not heard. Anytime that we sacrifice to give to the work of the Lord we are worshipping the Lord. Of course, gifts given for the purpose of being recognized by others or solely as a tax write-off would not be gifts of worship.

Giving

God told the Israelites that to bring the first fruits of their crops was a way they could worship Him. Deuteronomy 26:10, "And now, behold, I have brought the **firstfruits** of the land, which thou, O LORD, hast given me. And thou shalt set it before the LORD thy God, and **worship** before the LORD thy God."

Today we bring money, our tithes and offerings, to God's house as a means of worship, but monetary gifts are not the only type of giving mentioned with worship. I Chronicles 16:29 speaks of giving glory to God as worship. "**Give unto the LORD the glory due unto his name**: bring an offering, and come before him: **worship the LORD in the beauty of holiness**." Psalm 30:4 says, "Sing unto the LORD, O ye saints of his, and **give thanks** at the remembrance of his **holiness**." Be quick to give money, glory and thanks to the Lord. Give, not to be seen of others or just to meet a need, but give to worship.

Fearing the Lord

Psalm **96:9,** "O **worship** the LORD in the beauty of holiness: **fear before him**, all the earth." The fear the Lord is reverential trust with a hatred of evil. To fear the Lord is to believe that everything God says is true and everything He does is right and is for our good. We must fear Him if we are to worship Him. When we really fear the Lord we will have no problem praising the Lord.

Praise

II Chronicles 20:21, "And when he had consulted with the people, he appointed singers unto the LORD, and that should **praise the beauty of holiness**, as they went out before the army, and to say **Praise the LORD**; for his mercy endureth for ever." Psalm 99:5, "**Exalt** ye the LORD our God, and **worship** at his footstool: for he is **holy**." Psalm 99:9, "**Exalt** the LORD our God, and **worship** at his holy hill; for the LORD our God is **holy**." I find that to worship the Lord with praise helps me minimize my problems and gives me strength to face the trials of each day.

Going to God's House

When we think of worship we often think about going to church. The Sunday morning service in many churches is referred to as the worship service, but do we always really worship when we go to church? Do we give God our undivided attention? Many times our mind is on what is happening around us or on our plans for the coming week. We need to make a conscious effort to truly worship when we go to God's house.

A verse that we have already mentioned is Psalm 27:4, "One thing have I desired of the LORD, that will I seek after; that I may dwell in the **house of the LORD** all the days of my life, to behold the beauty of the LORD, and to enquire in **his temple**." In these wicked, sinful days it is more necessary than ever that we be faithful in God's house.

Hebrews 10:25, "Not forsaking the assembling of ourselves together, as the manner of some is; but exhorting one another; and **so much the more, as ye see the day approaching**." I believe we are living in the last days and we are approaching His return. Are you taking the time from your busy schedule to faithfully worship the Lord in your church? You need to be exhorted and encouraged by your pastor and church family and you need to do the same for them.

Humility

Many times in the Bible we read that the people bowed to worship. Nehemiah 8:6 is an example of this, "And Ezra blessed the LORD, the great God.
And all the people answered, Amen, Amen, with lifting up their hands: and they **bowed their heads, and worshipped the LORD with their faces to the ground**."

Bowing signifies humility. These people not only bowed their heads; they went further by putting their faces to the ground. Humility is a necessary requirement for true worship.

When we humble ourselves we take our eyes off of ourselves and center them on the Lord. We recognize how small and insignificant we are and how great and powerful God is. Humility is not an easy thing to attain because we are so self-centered and self-willed and it is difficult to let go of our pride.

God hates pride. Pride is a sin that we need to confess everyday if we are to have humility. It is so easy to fool ourselves into thinking that we are worshipping the Lord when in reality we are seeking to please ourselves and to receive the acclaim of others. Read the Proverbs regularly as they give good teaching concerning pride and humility.

Mary of Bethany is a good example of humility and worship. Every time the Scriptures mention her we find her bowed at Jesus' feet. In Luke 10 she **"sat at Jesus' feet"** and listened to Him proclaim His word. In John 11:32 **"she fell down at his feet,"** beseeching Him for her brother Lazarus who had died. In John 12 **"she anointed the feet of Jesus"** with costly ointment and wiped them with her hair.

She worshipped as she listened to His word, as she prayed for her brother, and as she offered her sacrificial gift to the Lord. These are all ways that we can worship the Lord today, but I find that even when I am doing these things I may only be going through the motions of worship.

There are days when I read my Bible and times when I go to church to hear God's Word, and yet I put down my Bible not knowing what I read or leave the church not knowing what I heard preached. That is not worship! There are days when I read every name on my prayer list but my heart is not truly concerned about the needs before me. That is not worship! There have been times when I have given my money or other gifts but I have done so grudgingly. That is not worship!

Praise the Lord, there are other times when I am so blessed as I read God's Word and times when I rejoice at what I have heard when I go to church. There are days when I pray with a burdened heart and weep over someone's needs. There are times when I delight in giving because I am doing so out of a heart filled with love for the Lord. These are acts of true worship!

How long has it been since you worshipped the Lord in the beauty of holiness?

Questions:

1. According to Rev. 4:11, why were we created? _____

2. What is the definition of worship given by my good friend, Carolyn Pace?
_____

3. What was one of the first things Noah did when he got off the ark?
_____

4. Rom. 1:25 warns about people who worship "the _____
more than the _____.

5. What is the sacrifice spoken of in Heb. 13:15? _____

6. What was the sacrifice mentioned in Phil. 4:18? _____

7. To bow the head is a sign of what? _____

8. Each time the Bible mentions Mary of Bethany where is she found?
_____

Lesson Five

"The Beautiful Queen"

"The Beautiful Queen"

"So shall the king greatly desire thy beauty; for he is thy Lord; and worship thou him." Psalm 45:11

The book of Esther gives a good illustration of what we have been studying about in the previous lessons of this study. The Jews, God's chosen people, had been taken into captivity in Persia, which was under the rule of King Ashasuerus. You are no doubt familiar with the account of King Ahasuerus' ridiculous command to Queen Vashti, and how that because she disobeyed him by refusing to parade her beauty before his princes and servants she was dethroned.

This created a need for a new queen and so his servants recommended in Esther 2:2-4, "Let there be fair young virgins sought for the king: and let the king appoint officers in all the provinces of his kingdom, that they may gather together all the fair young virgins unto Shushan the palace, to the house of the women, unto the custody of Hege the king's chamberlain, keeper of the women; and let their things for purification be given them: and let the maiden which pleaseth the king be queen instead of Vashti," The king liked this idea and made a decree to implement this plan.

Mordecai, one of the captive Jews, had taken as his daughter a young orphan maiden named Esther. When Mordecai heard the king's decree he saw this as a door of opportunity to free the Jews whose lives were in jeopardy. He brought Esther to the palace and placed her in the custody of Hegai, the king's chamberlain.

The Cleansing

Esther 2:9 tells us that, "The maiden pleased him, and she obtained kindness of him; and he speedily gave her things for **purification**, with such things as belonged to her, and seven maidens, which were meet to be given her, out of the king's house: and he preferred her and her maids unto the best place of the house of the women." Esther had been advised by Mordecai that she not reveal that she was Jewish, and every day he walked by the court of the women's house to see how she was doing.

To purify means to rid of impurities. Looking back to our discussion of the tabernacle in lesson three, we find in Exodus 30:18-19, that God told Moses, "Thou shalt also make a **laver of brass**......and thou shalt put water therein. For Aaron and his sons shall wash their hands and their feet thereat." God required the priests to be clean before they performed any ceremonies or sacrifices.

Just as Esther and the other maidens went through this time of purification to prepare themselves for King Ahasuerus we, too, must go through a cleansing to prepare ourselves for the King of Kings. We must first of all be washed in the Blood of the Lamb. Romans 5:8-9, "But God commendeth his love toward us, in that, while we were yet sinners, Christ died for us. Much more then, being now justified by his blood, we shall be saved from wrath though him." Revelation 1:5, "Unto him that loved us, and **washed us from our sins in his own blood**."

Secondly, we need the daily confessing of our sins to stay spiritually clean. David's prayer for cleansing is found in Psalm 51, and it a good pattern for us to use when we need forgiveness and cleansing. In verse 2 he says, "**Wash** me throughly from mine iniquity, and **cleanse** me from my sin." In verse 7 he goes on to say, "**Purge** me with hyssop, and I shall be **clean**: **wash** me, and I shall be whiter than snow." Again in verse 10 David writes, "Create in me a **clean heart**, O God; and renew a right spirit within me." Keep your sins confessed and your heart clean that you might be prepared to serve King Jesus.

The Anointing

For one year Esther and the other maidens prepared themselves for their appointment with the king. Their purification not only consisted of cleansing but also of anointing. Esther 2:12 tells us they were anointed for "six months with oil of myrrh, and six months with sweet odours, and other things for the **purifying** of the women."

Once again we refer back to the tabernacle where God told Moses to anoint Aaron and his sons as priests and to make a holy ointment from spices and **anoint** the tabernacle and its furnishings in order to sanctify it and make it holy. (Exodus 29:7-8; 30:22-33) In Song of Solomon 4:10 the bridegroom speaks of the anointing of his bride and says, "how much better is thy love than wine! and the smell of thine **ointments** than all spices!"

After the prophet Samuel anointed Saul to become the first king of Israel the Spirit of the Lord came upon Saul. (I Samuel 10:1, 6) Later, because of Saul's disobedience the Spirit of the Lord departed from Saul and God told Samuel to anoint David which Samuel did in I Samuel 16:13. "Then Samuel took the horn of oil and anointed him in the midst of his brethren: and the Spirit of the Lord came upon David from that day forward."

When we receive Christ as our Saviour the Holy Spirit comes to live in us and we need His anointing if we are to live a godly life. I John 2:27, "But the **anointing** which ye have received of him abideth in you..." As we empty ourselves of sin and self we are filled and anointed with the Spirit. Ephesians 5:18, "...be filled with the Spirit." Psalm 45:7, "Thou lovest righteousness, and hatest wickedness: therefore God, thy God, hath **anointed** thee with the oil of gladness above thy fellows." The anointing follows the cleansing. In some Christian circles today great emphasis is put on the anointing of the Holy Spirit but little is said about salvation or cleansing. God cannot fill a vessel that is already filled with sin.

The Adornment

When the time came for the maidens to go before the king they were given anything they desired to finish their preparation for this big occasion. Esther 2:15 tells us that when Esther's turn came "**she required nothing**." She must have been a young woman who possessed great natural beauty because even with no special adornment, she was favored by all who looked at her. Esther 2:17 says, "And the king loved Esther above all the women, and she obtained grace and favour in his sight more than all the virgins."

Unlike Esther, we have no natural holiness that makes us ready to stand before our Holy King. We read in Isaiah 64:6, "But we are all as an **unclean** thing, and all our righteousnesses are as **filthy rags**." If Esther would have presented herself to King Ahasuerus dressed in filthy rags she would no doubt have been rejected as queen. Since our Holy God demands holiness, and we are so unholy, can we ever be accepted by Him? Just as the maidens were offered any adornment they wanted, God has offered us a change of garments. When we get saved we trade in our filthy rags of self-righteousness for His robe of righteousness.

Isaiah 61:10, "I will greatly rejoice in the LORD, my soul shall be joyful in my God; for he hath clothed me with the **garments of salvation**, he hath covered me with the **robe of righteousness**, as a bridegroom decketh himself with ornaments, and as a bride adorneth herself with her jewels." Many people have done many good works and cannot believe that will not get them to heaven. The idea that salvation is free seems too easy—they think they must work for it. Titus 3:5 says, "Not by **works of righteousness** which we have done, but according to his mercy he saved us, by the washing of regeneration, and renewing of the Holy Ghost."

In Isaiah 61:3 the Lord has offered us some other exchanges of garments that we need to take advantage of. It says, "to give unto them **beauty** for ashes, the oil of **joy** for mourning, the **garment of praise** for the spirit of heaviness." We need not go through life discouraged, unhappy Christians when joy is available to us for the asking.

The Crown

Because Esther found favor in the eyes of King Ashasuerus we are told in Esther 2:17, "he set the **royal crown** upon her head and made her queen instead of Vashti."

She had accomplished what Mordecai had wished for—she was now the queen. We know the story of how the wicked Haman who had been promoted above all the princes had big plans for destroying the Jews. Mordecai hoped that Esther would have enough influence over the king to bring deliverance to God's people.

Even though Esther was the wife of the king she did not have the rights that we as wives have today. She told Mordecai in Esther 4:11, "All the king's servants, and the people of the king's provinces, do know, that whosoever, whether man or woman, shall come unto the king into the inner court, who is not called, there is one law of his to put him to death, except such to whom the king shall hold out the golden scepter, that he may live: but I have not been called to come in unto the king these thirty days." I am so glad that our God is not like King Ashasuerus and that through prayer I can have instant access to Him. His scepter is always extended to us.

Mordecai reminded Esther of the urgency to speak to the king. He said in Esther 4:13-14, "Think not with thyself that thou shalt escape in the king's house, more than all the Jews. For if thou altogether holdest thy peace at this time, then shall there enlargement and deliverance arise to the Jews from another place; but thou and thy father's house shall be destroyed: and who knoweth whether thou art come to the kingdom for such a time as this?" As a Jew, Esther had a calling to deliver her people and she decided to do so even if she lost her life, but she first asked Mordecai to have the Jews fast with her.

As Christians we, too, have a calling to tell our friends the good news of salvation that they might have the opportunity to be delivered from hell. Esther risked her life to save her people; are we willing to be embarrassed in order to bring our friends to salvation?

To make a long story short, Esther was granted a hearing with the king and invited him and Haman to a banquet that she had prepared. They agreed and came to the banquet, but when the king asked about her petition she must have gotten cold feet, for instead of revealing her petition she invited them to another banquet. This tells me that Esther was human just as I am. How many times have I gotten cold feet when I wanted to witness to someone?

God gave her another chance and at the second banquet the king asked again in Esther 7:2, "What is thy petition, queen Esther? and it shall be granted thee: and what is thy request? and it shall be performed, even to the half of the kingdom." Esther revealed her identity, her petition was granted, Mordecai was honored, Haman was hanged on the gallows that he had prepared for Mordecai, the Jews were spared from destruction, and many people in the land became Jews as a result. God won the victory!

We need to be faithful to our calling just as Esther was. Because she was willing to follow Mordecai's leading she received her crown and saved her nation. We are told in the New Testament of some crowns that we as Christians can receive if we will faithfully follow Christ's leading in our lives.

Incorruptible Crown
I Corinthians 9:25, "And every man that striveth for the mastery is temperate in all things. Now they do it to obtain a corruptible crown; but we an **incorruptible**." The dictionary defines incorruptible as "that cannot be corrupted; that cannot be bribed; not liable to decay or destruction." When the Lord gives us something He gives us the best!

Crown of Rejoicing
I Thessalonians 2:19, "For what is our hope, or joy, or **crown of rejoicing**? Are not even ye in the presence of our Lord Jesus Christ at his coming?" Paul is speaking of those that he has won to the Lord. We will be rewarded for the souls that we have won to Christ with a crown of rejoicing.

Crown of Righteousness
II Timothy 4:8, "Henceforth there is laid up for me a **crown of righteousness**, which the Lord, the righteous judge, shall give me at that day: and not to me only, but unto all them also that love his appearing." We are sometimes so involved with our daily activities that we forget that the Lord is going to return. It may be today! Are you awaiting His coming?

Crown of Life

James 1:12, "Blessed is the man that endureth temptation: for when he is tried, he shall receive the **crown of life**, which the Lord hath promised to them that love him." Temptations are all around us, but if we really love the Lord it will be much easier to endure temptation because we will want to please the One we love. When we love Him and stay close to Him, He will change our desires from that of sinful pleasures to that of pleasing Him.

The Bible uses the word temptation to include more than being tempted to sin-- it can also be speaking of trials and tribulations. Revelation 2:10 is an example of this, "Fear none of those things which thou shalt suffer: behold, the devil shall cast some of you into prison, that ye may be tried; and ye shall have tribulation ten days: be thou faithful unto death, and I will give thee a **crown of life**." Once again if we really love the Lord and stay close to Him we can endure the trials He allows to come our way and be faithful unto Him, knowing that the reward is greater than the trial.

Crown of Glory
I Peter 5:4, "And when the chief Shepherd shall appear, ye shall receive a **crown of glory** that fadeth not away." If we look back to verse two, we see that this crown is given to those who "feed the flock of God" which would be those who teach God's Word to other Christians. As women we do not pastor a church or preach, but if you have ever taught a Sunday School class you instructed a friend about spiritual matter, you are eligible to receive this crown.

Guard your crown so that it won't be taken from you. Revelation 3:11, "Behold, I come quickly: hold that fast which thou hast, **that no man take thy crown**." Some people might say they don't want any rewards for their service for the Lord. While this might sound like humility, it is not scriptural.

We should want as many crowns as we can possibly earn, because Revelation 4:10-11 tells us what we will do with our crowns when we get to heaven. "The four and twenty elders fall down before him that sat on the throne, and **worship** him that liveth for ever and ever, and cast their **crowns** before the throne, saying, Thou art worthy, O Lord, to receive glory and honour and power: for thou hast created all things, and for thy pleasure they are and were created."

Will you have any crowns to place at His feet?

Questions:

1. What function did the laver of brass have in the tabernacle? (Exo. 30:18-19)
   _____

2. How long did Esther and the other maidens prepare themselves for their meeting with the king? _____

3. Isa. 64:6 tells us that all of our righteousness is as what?
   _____

4. When we get saved we receive the garment of _____ and the robe of _____. (Isa, 61:10)

5. We exchange ashes for _____, mourning for _____, the spirit of heaviness _____.

6. Name the five crowns that Christians can obtain?
   (a) _____ (b)
   _____ (c)
   _____ (d)
   _____ (e)
   _____

7. Rev. 3:11 warns us, "hold that fast which thou hast, that no man take _____."

8. Memorize Rev. 4:11

Lesson Six

"I'm Coming! Are You Ready?"

"I'm Coming! Are You Ready?"

"...for the marriage of the Lamb is come, and his wife hath made herself ready." Revelation 19:7

Recently my daughter sent me an email entitled "I'm coming." When I opened the email the page consisted of only three words; "are you ready?" My first thought was that my daughter was making a surprise visit, but when I talked to her on the phone she laughed and told me to look at the email again because there was an attachment that I had failed to open.

Of course, I was disappointed that my daughter was not coming to see us, but the attachment contained pictures and told of a much more important event that could take place at any time. We read about this event in I Thessalonians 4:16-17, "For the Lord himself shall descend from heaven with a shout, with the voice of the archangel, and with the trump of God: and the dead in Christ shall rise first: then we which are alive and remain shall be **caught up** together with them in the clouds, to meet the Lord in the air: and so shall we ever be with the Lord."

Why do I believe that this event could take place at any time? Because God's Word tells us what to expect in the last days before Christ returns, and the description given in II Timothy 3:1-5 certainly sounds like what is happening in the world today. "This know also, that in the **last days perilous times shall come**. For men shall be lovers of their own selves, covetous, boasters, proud, blasphemers, disobedient to parents, unthankful, unholy, without natural affection, trucebreakers, false accusers, incontinent, fierce, despisers of those that are good, traitors, heady, highminded, lovers of pleasures more than lovers of God; having a form of godliness, but denying the power thereof: from such turn away."

Because so many years have passed since this prophecy was given, many people doubt that Christ will return and others actually deny His second coming. II Peter 3:3-4 predicted that this would happen; "Knowing this first, that there shall come in the last days scoffers, walking after their own lusts, and saying, **Where is the promise of his coming?** for since the fathers fell asleep, all things continue as they were from the beginning of the creation."

Verses 8-10 go on to say, "But, beloved, be not ignorant of this one thing, that one day is with the Lord as a thousand years, and a thousand years as one day. The Lord is not slack concerning his **promise**, as some men count slackness; but is longsuffering to us-ward, not willing that any should perish, but that all should come to repentance. But the day of **the Lord will come** as a thief in the night."

Even Christians have lost sight of this all-important event and this surely has contributed to the unholy lives that many professing Christians are living today. Our prayer should be the words Paul wrote in II Thessalonians 3:5, "And the Lord direct your hearts into the **love of God**, and into the **patient waiting for Christ**." The love of God and the patient waiting for Christ go hand in hand. When we love someone, we desire to be near that one.

The Bridegroom!

In the summer of 1960, I was at home in Ohio taking classes at the University of Cincinnati, working on my teaching degree. That same summer, my fiancée, Bert Singletary, was in Pensacola, Florida, where he pastored a church. Because I was in love, I looked forward with great anticipation to a day in August when he would come to Ohio and we would be married. As I waited for him to come I was not sitting around doing nothing, but rather I was making preparations for that special day.

In 1960, the ordinary wedding was not as elaborate as it is today, and since my dad was a Baptist preacher there was not a lot of money to spend on the wedding, but I did everything I could to make it a very special occasion. My mother made me a beautiful dress and a lady in our church baked a delicious cake. Though it seemed so far away, the day of his arrival, Tuesday, August 16, finally came. How excited I was!

Would you believe that he forgot the wedding ring and had to have someone mail it him? There was no overnight delivery as there is today, but the ring did arrive by Friday, August 19, which was our wedding day. It is still exciting for me to look back and remember the events of that day so many years ago, but how much more exciting it should be for me to look forward to the coming of Christ and the great wedding day that awaits me—the **marriage of the Lamb**.

Just as I prepared myself to look my best for Bert's arrival, and as Esther prepared herself to meet King Ahasuerus, so should we, as the bride make special preparations for the coming of Christ, our Bridegroom. Revelation 19:7, "Let us be glad and rejoice, and give honour to him: for the **marriage of the Lamb** is come, and his wife hath **made herself ready**."

Are you looking forward to the day when Christ will return or have you become complacent in your preparation for His return? Matthew 24:44, "Therefore be ye also ready: for in such an hour as ye think not the Son of man cometh."

The Bride Wore White!

Customs have changed since I got married in 1960. In those days it was considered improper to be married in a white dress if you were not a virgin. That is no longer true. Today women who have been married numerous times have big weddings, and never think twice about wearing a white gown. While this "anything goes" attitude toward marriage may be accepted in society today, God's Word tells us that Christ requires His bride, to be clean and holy.

We read in II Corinthians 11:2, "For I am jealous over you with godly jealousy: for I have espoused you to one husband, that I may present you as a **chaste virgin** to Christ." Revelation 19:8 says, "And to her was granted that she should be arrayed in **fine linen**, **clean** and **white**: for the fine linen is the **righteousness** of saints."

In Ephesians 5:25-27 we read, "Husbands love your wives, even as Christ also loved the church, and gave himself for it; that he might **sanctify** and **cleanse** it with the washing of water by the word. That he might present it to himself a glorious church, not having spot, or wrinkle, or any such thing; but that it should be **holy** and without blemish."

When we are saved He clothes us in His righteousness. Keep your garments clean by confessing your sins and washing yourselves in His word regularly. I John 2:28, "And now, little children, abide in him; that, when he shall appear, we may have confidence, and not be ashamed before him at his coming."

First Love!

If you have ever been in love, take a moment to reflect on those days when your love was young and new. Do you remember how you wanted to spend every spare moment with the one you loved? No doubt, you wanted to look your very best when you knew he was coming to see you. You didn't want him to see you with curlers in your hair. You wanted to do special things that you knew would please him. You may even have been willing to sacrifice something that you really wanted so that you could afford a special gift for him.

After being married for a number of years we sometimes take our mate for granted and neglect doing some of the things we used to do. If your marriage has become boring and your love has grown cold, maybe you need to make an effort to renew some of those acts of first love.

What about your love for the Saviour, has it also grown cold? As John wrote about the seven churches in the book of Revelation, he praised the church of Ephesus for their good works, their patience and their hatred of evil, but he reprimanded them in Revelation 2:4 saying, "Nevertheless I have somewhat against thee, because thou hast left thy **first love**." He told them in verse five to "**repent**, and do the **first works**, or else I will come unto thee quickly, and remove thy candlestick out of his place, except thou repent." One of the signs of Christ's coming given in Matthew 24:12 are, "the **love of many shall wax cold**."

In Jeremiah 2:2-3 the Lord speaks to the Israelites, about how they had forgotten their love for Him. "Thus saith the LORD; I remember thee, the **kindness** of thy youth, the **love** of thine espousals, when thou wentest after me in the wilderness......Israel was **holiness** unto the LORD," In verse seven he says, "And I brought you into a plentiful country, to eat the fruit thereof and the goodness thereof; but when ye entered, ye **defiled** my land, and made mine heritage an abomination."

The Lord did not write this to the heathen, but to His chosen people. In verse nine he says, "Wherefore I will yet plead with you" and in verse 13, "For my people have committed two evils; they have **forsaken me** the fountain of living waters, and hewed them out cisterns, broken cisterns, that can hold no water." The Israelites had forsaken God, the living water of life, and dug useless cisterns that held no water. Are we any different from the Israelites? Are we putting our efforts into building cisterns that hold no water when we could be spending time with Christ,
the Living Water?

In Ezekiel 16, we read the parable of the faithless wife, which once again is speaking of the nation of Israel. These verses bring to mind the things we discussed about Queen Esther—the purification, the anointing and the adornment.

The Lord said in verses 8-15, "Now when I passed by thee, and looked upon thee, behold, thy time was the **time of love**; and I spread my skirt over thee...I sware unto thee, and entered into a covenant with thee.....and thou becamest mine. Then **washed**

I thee with water; yea, I **throughly washed** away thy blood from thee, and I **anointed** thee with oil. I **clothed** thee also with broidered work......and I girded thee about with **fine linen**, and I covered thee with **silk**. I decked thee also with **ornaments**, and I put **bracelets** upon thy hands, and a **chain** on thy neck. And I put a **jewel** on thy forehead, and **earrings** in thine ears, and a **beautiful crown** upon thine head. Thus wast thou decked with **gold and silver**; and thy raiment was of **fine linen, and silk, and broidered work**....and thou wast exceeding **beautiful**, and thou didst prosper into a kingdom. And thy renoun went forth among the heathen for thy **beauty**: for it was perfect through my comeliness, which I had put upon thee.....**But thou didst trust in thine own beauty**, and playedest the harlot...."

This grieved the Lord and He said in verse 43, "Because thou hast not **remembered** the days of thy youth, but hast fretted me in all these things; behold, therefore I also will **recompense** thy way upon thine head..." Just as the Lord was disappointed that the Israelites had forgotten His covenant and gone their own way, is He not also disappointed and pained by our indifference and lack of holiness?

Any woman in her right mind would not be willing to share the love of her husband with that of another woman. So the Lord does not want to share our love for Him with our love for the world. I John 2:15, "Love not the world, neither the things that are in the world. **If any man love the world, the love of the Father is not in him**. The Lord wants our wholehearted love. Matthew 22:37-38, "Thou shalt **love** the Lord thy God with **all thy heart**, and with **all thy soul**, and with **all thy mind**. This is the first and great commandment." John 14:15 says, "If ye **love** me, **keep my commandments**."

The Ten Virgins!

In Matthew 25:1-13 we read the parable of the ten virgins. "Then shall the kingdom of heaven be likened unto ten virgins, which took their lamps, and went forth to meet the bridegroom. And **five** of them were **wise**, and **five** were **foolish**. they that were foolish took their lamps, and took no oil with them: but the wise took oil in their vessels with their lamps. While the bridegroom tarried, they all slumbered and slept. And at midnight there was a cry made, Behold, the **bridegroom cometh**; go ye out to meet him. Then all those virgins arose, and trimmed their lamps. And the foolish said unto the wise, Give us of your oil; for our lamps are gone out. But the wise answered, saying, Not so; lest there be not enough for us and you: but go ye rather to them that sell, and buy for yourselves. And while they went to buy, the bridegroom came; and they that were ready went in with him to the marriage: and the door was shut. Afterward came also the other virgins, saying, Lord, Lord, open to us. But he answered and said, Verily I say unto you, I know you not. **Watch therefore**, for ye know neither the day nor the hour wherein the Son of man cometh."

Most Christians believe that Christ is coming again but many are like the five foolish virgins who had taken no oil in their vessels to refill their lamps. The oil is symbolic of the Holy Spirit who comes to live in us when we get saved. Is the oil in your lamp getting low because you are nonchalant about your relationship with the Holy Spirit? Is your lamp burning so dimly that your friends don't even know you are a Christian?

Are you ready for the bridegroom?

Are you worshipping the Lord in the beauty of holiness?

Questions:

1. According to I Thess. 4:16, when the trump of God sounds, who will rise first?
   _____

2. Who is the bridegroom at the marriage of the Lamb? (Rev. 19:7)
   _____

3. Who is the bride? _____

4. In Rev. 19:8, what does the fine linen, clean and white represent?
   _____

5. What was the one thing wrong with the church at Ephesus in Rev. 2:4?
   _____

6. What is one of the signs of the second coming given in Matt. 24:12
   _____

7. How are we to love the Lord? (Matt. 22:37) _____
   _____

8. In the parable of the ten virgins given in Matt. 25, how many were wise?
   _____

9. Why were the other virgins called foolish? _____

10. Why does Matt. 25:13 tell us to watch? _____
    _____

32779718R00032

Made in the USA
San Bernardino, CA
16 April 2016